Contents

Name: ____

1 Your handwriting folder

Design a cover for your handwriting folder. Think about the layout and whether you should use print or joined handwriting. You might decorate the Title box or some of the capital letters used.

2 Decorative patterns

Here are some patterns that you might use to decorate your work.
Try these first and then design some patterns of your own.

3 Borders and line patterns

Create a page of borders and line patterns that you might use to decorate your work. Store them in your handwriting folder.

4 Decorating letters

These capital letters illustrate different styles and decoration.
Draw each letter in a box in a different style and decorate them all.

O Q S V Y

5 Label your folders

Design some eye-catching labels to use in your folders at school and at home. Here are some subject folders you might label.

Think about this!

Think carefully about which words should have a capital letter at the beginning.
Some of the writing is in speech.
How will you show this?

Stories I have started

Stuff from the internet

My birthday book

The best football team ever!

My favourite poem

List of good websites

Words I need for writing

Information I may need again

The greatest pop group in the world

6 Some words you should know

Write the words in the box in alphabetical order.
Then practise reading and spelling them with your partner.

Think about this!

Write each word at least three times.
Try not to lift your pen off the paper until you have finished writing the word.
When you have finished, try writing each word again with your eyes closed.

happy children baby garden heard birthday
clothes balloon head brother great

7 Some words you should know

Write the words in the box in alphabetical order.
Then practise reading and spelling them with your partner.

Think about this!

Write each word at least three times.
Try not to lift your pen off the paper until you have finished writing the word.
When you have finished, try writing each word again with your eyes closed.

world clause acronym swimming preposition
those something rhetorical synonym word
sure work quotation

8 Greetings!

Greetings cards may be sent on many occasions. Here are some typical greetings. Copy them out and store them in your handwriting folder for future use. Remember: these are exclamations!

Happy Birthday!

Happy Anniversary!

Get Well Soon!

I'm Sorry!

Congratulations!

Sorry You're Leaving!

A New Baby!

Just a Note!

Think about this!

Many people are especially pleased to receive a greetings card made by hand instead of bought. It is often a good idea to make these in advance so that you have one ready for a special occasion.
Design a greetings card for a special occasion that will soon happen. Then you will be ready and save money!

9 Design some labels

People use decorative lettering to label items in the home.
Design some labels for the herbs, spices and condiments below.

Rosemary

Marjoram

Salt

Pepper

Sugar

Thyme

Basil

Oregano

Coriander

Parsley

Ginger

Think about this!

All sorts of things at school and in the home need labels. You might design some labels to help someone keep tools or gardening equipment in order. Some or all of your labels can be illustrated.

10 Beware the apostrophe!

Like the dot on the letter "i", apostrophes can escape from their correct position, especially when we write in a hurry. Some apostrophes in the sentences below are wrongly placed; others are missing completely. Rewrite each sentence, putting each apostrophe in the correct place.

Think about this!

Before you begin, write out three rules to remind yourself:

1. What is the rule for a contraction?
2. What is the rule if the possessor is singular?
3. What is the rule if the possessor is plural?

1. I ca'nt find my book and my pencil.

2. The boys' knee was badly grazed when he fell.

3. If I were you, I would'nt go out tonight.

4. Smoke was drifting from the houses chimney's.

5. "We were'nt there," said the boys to the police officer.

6. Its a tool for taking stone's out of horse's hoove's.

11 Spelling tips

Here are some well-known mnemonics for spelling.
Write a sentence to illustrate each one.

Think about this!

These are all useful rules for spelling. They are often called mnemonics.
You might want to write these and any other tips that you know, on a page in your Handwriting folder to help you remember these rules for spelling.

1. *When two vowels go walking, the first one does the talking.*

2. *"i" before "e" except after "c".*

3. *Remember: there's a rat in separate!*

4. *Possess possesses a posse of "esses".*

5. *Friday is your friend because it's the end of the week.*

6. *Necessary: one coffee, two sugars!*

12 Correct the errors

Each of these sentences contains at least one spelling error.
Write the sentences correctly in your best handwriting.

1. He saw a heard of buffalos approaching across the plane.

2. We had a grate thyme at the party last weak.

3. The night was covered from head to tow in steal armour.

4. The cake was maid with self-razing flower.

13 Writing in italics

The extract below is written in an italic style. Try writing some of the words in italics. Then write the quote in your own style.

Be not afraid of greatness. Some are born great, some achieve greatness, and some have greatness thrust upon 'em.

William Shakespeare (Twelfth Night, Act 2 Scene 5)

Think about this!

Italic writing looks very attractive but needs a lot of care. Sometimes it is used to highlight a particular word. Other ways to highlight your writing include underlining or **enlarging** words. Write a proverb or saying using one of these techniques to highlight certain words.

14 Handwriting check 1: "Song of the Witches"

Write this poem in your best handwriting. You might wish to decorate your poem in a suitable way.

Double, double, toil and trouble,
Fire burn, and cauldron bubble.

Fillet of fenny snake,
In the cauldron boil and bake.
Eye of newt and toe of frog,
Wool of bat and tongue of dog,
Adder's fork and blind-worm's sting,
Lizard's leg and owlet's wing,
For a charm of powerful trouble,
Like a hell-broth boil and bubble.

Double, double, toil and trouble,
Fire burn and cauldron bubble.
Cool it with a baboon's blood,
Then the charm is firm and good.

William Shakespeare (Macbeth, Act 4 Scene 1)

15 Writing dialogue in plays

The dialogue below is from the opening scene of Shakespeare's "Macbeth".
Use it as a guide to help you write a script for the play.

Think about this!

You might wish to use a copy of "Macbeth" as a reference.
Sometimes the stage directions and scene are written in italics.
Remember, dialogue in a play is a bit like poetry: each new line starts with a capital letter.
See if you can find the word used when several actors exit the stage at the same time. You might also make some drawings to help the costume designer and the set designer.

Macbeth

Act 1, Scene 1: A deserted heath. Thunder and lightning.
Enter three witches.

First witch: When shall we three meet again?
In thunder, lightning, or in rain?
Second witch: When the hurly-burly's done,
When the battle's lost and won.
Third witch: That will be ere the set of sun.
First witch: Where the place?
Second witch: Upon the heath.
Third witch: There to meet with Macbeth.
First witch: I come, Grimalkin.
Second witch: Paddock calls.
Third witch: Anon.
All: Fair is foul, and foul is fair,
Hover through the fog and filthy air.

Then they exit.

16 Design a menu

Use the menu below to help you to set out a menu as if your house was a famous restaurant. You might include all your favourite foods! Use both print and joined writing in your menu.

Think about this!

Collect together some menus from restaurants and takeaways. Look at how different fonts and type-styles have been used to create a visual effect. Experiment with some different fonts on a computer.

Notre Maison

Starter:	Avocado Surprise
Fish course:	Seafood Melody
Main course:	Roast Topside of Beef Yorkshire Pudding served with Roast Potatoes, Carrots and Cauliflower
Dessert:	Lemon Meringue Pie with Fresh Cream

Coffee and Mints

17 Design a card for a special festival

We send cards to mark special festivals throughout the year.
Below are some of the festivals you might wish to celebrate.

New Year   Christmas   Eid-ul-Fitr   Hannukah
Diwali   Easter   Thanksgiving   Yuan Tan
Al-Hijra   Rosh Hashanah

Find out when some of the major religious festivals are held and which religions they belong to.
You may wish to mark the major festivals on a calendar, but remember that some occur at different times in different years.

18 Planning a front cover for a book

Decorative lettering and illustrations are often used on front covers, as the example below shows. Answer the questions on this page to help you plan the design of a front cover for a schoolbook (see sheet 19).

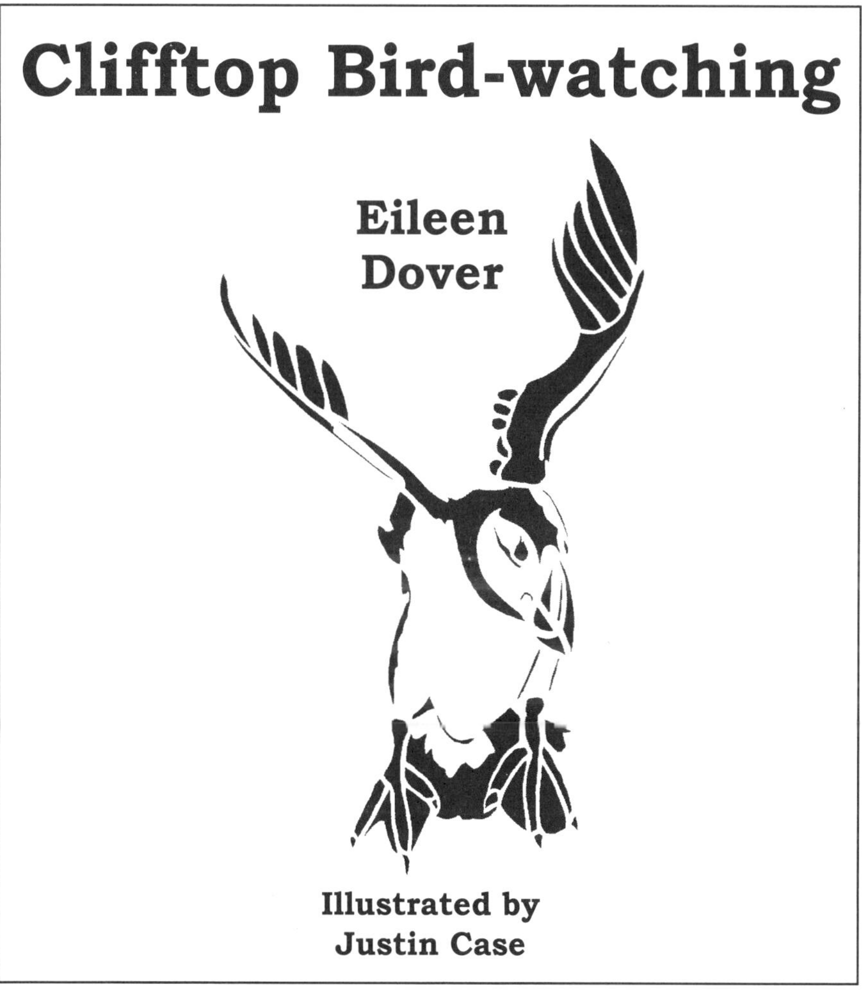

1. What title will you give your book?
2. How big should the book title be?
3. How big will you make the title box?
4. Which will appear first, the title of the book or the name of the author?
5. Is your book part of a series? If yes, what is the series title?
6. Does anything on the front cover say what age group your book is aimed at?

19 Design a front cover for a schoolbook

Gather together a selection of schoolbooks for different subjects.
Choose your favourite subject and design a new front cover for the schoolbook.
Before you begin, think about your answers to the questions on sheet 18.

Design your own school logo

A logo is an emblem used as a badge. Using the examples below as templates, design and colour a new logo for your school.

Think about this!

What image would you use to represent your school?
Could you use your school's initials in your logo design?
Can your logo design include any school colours?

21 Roots and derivations

Link each root word listed below to its possible derivations. Add any other derivations that you know. You may need to use a dictionary.

Think about this!

You may set out your links in different ways. You might use arrows, dashes or brackets to link the words.
If you make a list, think about punctuation. Will you use a colon, semi-colons, commas?

Root words

medical sign explain social physics secret

Derivations

medicine medication signal signature explanation explanatory society anti-social physician physiotherapy secrete secretion

22 Idiomatic sayings

Idiomatic sayings are not meant to be taken literally.
Write each of these idiomatic sayings four times, as quickly as you can.
You might think about how you would illustrate each saying.

Don't beat about the bush.

Put a brave face on it.

Don't dwell on it.

It's no use crying over spilt milk.

23 Correct the errors

Each of these sentences contains at least one spelling error.
Write the sentences correctly in your best handwriting.

1. Put your coat over theyre.

2. Their are fairies at the bottom of there garden.

3. They forgot to take there homework with them.

4. Behind every dark cloud theirs a silver lining.

24 Make the adverb

Make each of the words in the box into an adverb, writing a sentence to illustrate the meaning of each word.

Think about this!

An **adjective** is a word added to a noun to add quality to its meaning.
Now write a definition of an **adverb**.

hopeful timid excited grumpy angry hurried
silent fretful slow happy apologetic fearful

An adverb is ____________________

25 Design a poster

Use the template below to help you design a poster (or flyer) inviting guests to a Parents' Evening at your school. Don't forget to include the date, place and time, what they will see, and something to encourage them to attend.

Please come to our Parents' Evening

at

Boscombe Road Primary School

on

Thursday 15th October at 7.30pm

We have worked hard to set out all of our work for you to see.

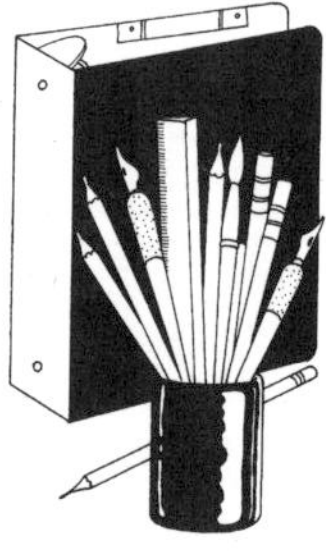

Tea, coffee and other refreshments will be served in the Hall.

26 A speed writing test

Write the following tongue-twister as many times as you can in one minute.
You may need a clock or a watch to time yourself!

Peter Piper picked a peck of pickled pepper.
Where is the peck of pickled pepper Peter Piper picked?

Think about this!

When you have finished your speed test, write the tongue-twister again, but this time with your eyes closed! Next, write another tongue-twister to make a speed test for your partner or a friend.

27 Match the prefix

Add the correct prefix to each of the words in the second box.
Write each new word three times.
There are clues to four new words in the illustrations!

tele circum auto uni trans

form vision rotate vent communication atlantic
cycle stance biography corn

28 Match the suffix

able and *ible*

Add the correct suffix to each of the words in the box.
Write each new word three times.
What spelling rules apply to those words ending in a single "e"?

depend flex prefer exhaust think suggest agree
reverse profit corrupt like response value sense
desire digest advise

29 Correct the errors

Each of the following sentences contains at least one spelling error.
Write the sentences correctly, in your best handwriting.

Dr Jeckyl worked in his laboratery.

The bus hit a stationery lorrey.

The funerral moved on to the cemetory.

The General survayed the territary.

Sweats and cake are known as confectionry.

He dictated notes to his secretry.

30 AttenSHUN!

Each of the words in the second box can be altered to take one of the "shun"-sounding endings in the first box. Write the new words in alphabetical order, each with the correct ending.

sion tian tion

Mars erode collect tense divide inspect fuse add
manse complicate multiply reduce depress
quest predict rash

31 Different writing styles

Write these sentences in different styles to create an impact.

Stop! Children crossing.

Beware of the Dog!

Trespassers will be prosecuted!

Keep off the grass!

32 Handwriting check 2: "Cats"

Write this poem in your best handwriting.
You might wish to decorate your copy in a suitable way.

Cats

Cats sleep
Anywhere,
Any table,
Any chair,
Top of piano,
Window-ledge,
In the middle,
On the edge,

Open drawer,
Empty shoe,
Anybody's
Lap will do.
Fitted in a
cardboard box,
In the cupboard
With your frocks
Anywhere!
They don't care!
Cats sleep
Anywhere.

Eleanor Farjeon

33 Onomatopoeic words

Write the words in the box below in ways that make them more visually dramatic.

Think about this!

You could enlarge, *italicise*, l-e-n-g-t-h-e-n or squeeze a word to highlight it.
You could make a word shape or use colour to add extra impact.

splash plop zoom zip crunch ooze squelch shudder trickle shunt crackle

34 Labelling road signs

Different-shaped signs at the side of the road use letters, words and illustrations to give drivers information about what is ahead. What do you think these signs tell drivers? Write a label beneath each one.

35 Designing road signs

Using the shapes below, design some road signs of your own. You can add symbols and words to each sign. Use capital letters for added impact. You may colour your road signs, if you wish.

36 Pictograms

Each of these Chinese pictograms represents a word or words. Be careful when you copy them: an extra line might alter the meaning! Design your own pictograms and see if your partner can guess what they represent.

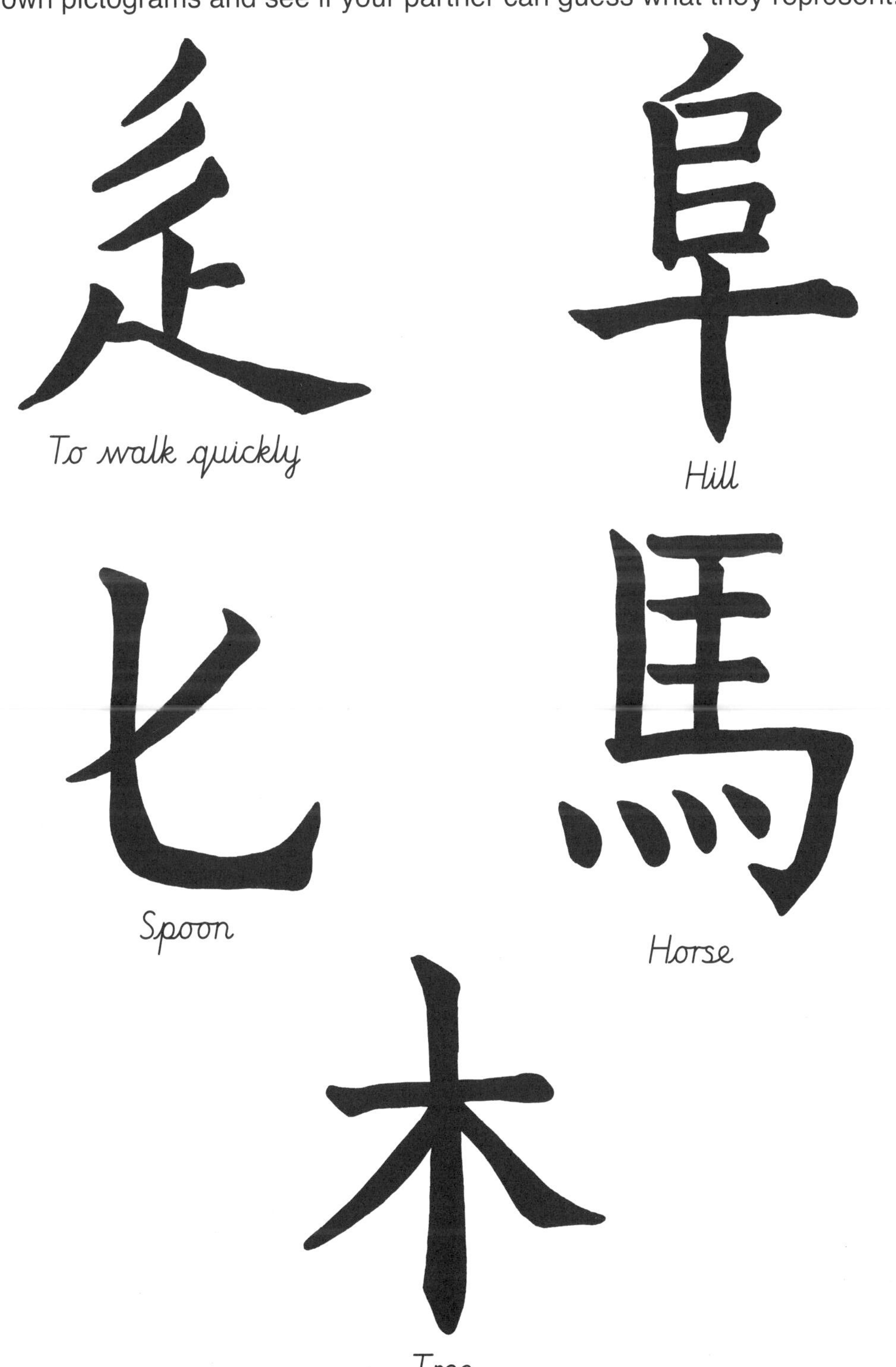

37 Writing a list

It is often useful to have a list of books you may want to read or refer to again. This sheet gives you one idea of how to keep a list. You may want to store it in your handwriting folder.

BOOK TITLE	AUTHOR	PUBLISHER	ISBN

38 Proverbs and sayings

Design an illustration for each of the following sayings and write the proverb underneath as a caption.

We pushed the boat out.

We burnt the candle at both ends.

Now we must face the music.

Think about this!

These proverbs and sayings are not intended to be taken literally; they have a double meaning. We use them to make a point.
Think about how you might illustrate this one: "Too many cooks spoil the broth."

39 Handwriting check 3: "Hints on pronunciation"

Write this poem in your best handwriting.

I take it you already know
Of though, and bough, and cough and dough?
Others may stumble, but not you
On hiccough, thorough, laugh and through.
Well done! And now you wish, perhaps,
To learn of less familiar traps.

Beware of heard, a dreadful word
That looks like beard and sounds like bird.
And dead: it's said like bed, not bead
For goodness sake don't call it "deed"!
Watch out for meat, and great, and threat,
(They rhyme with suite, and straight and debt);

A moth is not a moth in mother,
Nor both in bother, broth in brother,
And here is not a match for there,
Nor dear and fear for bear and pear,
And then there's dose and rose and lose
Just look these up and goose and choose.

And cork and work, and card and ward,
And font and front, and word and sword,
And do and go, and thwart and cart
Come, come, I've hardly made a start!
A dreadful language? Man alive.
I'd mastered it when I was five.

Anon

40 Do you have an "ology"?

Words ending in "ology" often mean the study of something.
Write a sentence explaining the meaning of each of the words in the box.
For example: Astrology is the study of the supposed influence of the stars and planets on our futures.

Biology Sociology Ecology Zoology Toxicology
Astrology Physiology Meteorology
Criminology Geology

41 Some words you should know

Write the words in the box in alphabetical order.
Then practise reading and spelling them with your partner.

Think about this!

Write each word at least three times.
Try not to lift your pen off the paper until you have finished writing the word.
When you have finished, try writing each word again with your eyes closed.

paper own window lady friends sound whole
earth sister money white important why father

42 A speed writing test

Many years ago, children who misbehaved in class were asked to write out lines, such as the ones below, 100 times! Write the first example as often as you can in one minute. (You may need to use a clock or a watch.) Think about how long it would take you to write it 100 times – and how tired your writing hand would be!

I must pay attention in class.

Children should be seen and not heard.

Think about this!

When you have finished your speed test, write the instruction again, but this time with your eyes closed! Next, write the second instruction to make a speed test for your partner or a friend.

43 Some words you should know

Write the words in the box in alphabetical order.
Then practise reading and spelling them with your partner.

Think about this!

Write each word at least three times.
Try not to lift your pen off the paper until you have finished writing the word.
When you have finished, try writing each word again with your eyes closed.

comma idiom metaphor slang colon imagery
adjective cliche simile directive adverb quotation
ellipsis apostrophe proverb article

44 Silent letters

Write the words in the box in alphabetical order and as many times as you can on one line. Underline the silent letter in each word.

ghost comb autumn bomber reign rhythm
knives hymn thumb calm solemn mnemonic
debt sign calf glisten

Now write the silent letter in each of the words:

45 Handwriting check 4: "Skateboarder"

Write this poem in your best handwriting.
You might wish to decorate your copy in a suitable way.

I can soar, I can swoop,
I can buckle at will,
I've tried looping the loop,
I've touched fifty downhill.

I've done end-over-end,
I've shot into the sky,
I zoom down, then ascend,
Gravity I defy.

I am flirting with death
As I hang there in space,
I am holding my breath
For I'm winning this race.

I am moving so fast
That my vision is blurred.
I am flying at last.
I'm a bird! I'm a bird!

Charles Connell

46 Handwriting check 5: Proverbs and sayings

In years gone by, people used proverbs and simple rhymes to help them live better and more healthy lives. Write these proverbs and sayings in your best handwriting, then see if you can find some more examples.

Early to bed and early to rise
Makes a man healthy, wealthy and wise.

After dinner, sit awhile;
After supper, walk a mile.

An apple a day keeps
the doctor away.

If you iron tonic need,
Eat more spinach, beet and swede;
If your nerves are all awry,
Lettuces and onions try.

47

Handwriting check 6: "I love to do my homework"

And finally! Write this poem in your best handwriting and keep it in your handwriting folder. Do you think what the poem says is too good to be true?

I love to do my homework,
It makes me feel so good.
I love to do exactly
As my teacher says I should

I love to do my homework,
I never miss a day.
I even love the men in white
Who are taking me away.

Anon